1

FOREWORD

The closer I get to my dream, the greater the challenges are with my walk with God.

These demonic spirits challenge everything that I am and everything that I plan to be. They want me to lose focus of my goals, so that my dream will continue as only A DREAM! Well today I can honestly say that my dream is no longer just a dream....

My Harsh truth...
By Zachery A. Hoagland

The First Chapter

With just days left before I take one of the biggest steps of my life, I find myself cruising through the town that raised me. While cruising my I-Phone clicks in that I have an Uber pick-up that was only minutes away.

This customer chose to ride as a Pool trip! A pool trip for those that have no knowledge; Is when a customer accepts a ride with another customer for a cheaper rate. Mind you reader, a cheaper rate can be $1.00 difference in their bill!

But the catch is; There's a chance that you will be taking a trip around the world before making it to your destination. (Figuratively reader!) But there's a catch 22 for this rate.

"Hello Sir, how are you? And happy late New Year's" I greeted the customer.

"Howdy, can you take this turn here? I have very little time to get to my destination." He whispered.

Reader I've been in this situation countless times. Yes I heard his request, but my eyes were focused on the name at the bottom of the screen of my phone.

My screen read Cindy. (If you recall reader, I greeted the customer as Sir.) So, this was a clear indicator that another trip had been added to my route.

Needless to say, I ignored this guy and continued to drive. But he became a little more aggressive in his approach.

"Driver I need you to take the next turn Please. I'm running late for my flight."

"Sir, I have another trip to pick up." I told him.

"Another trip!" He snarled. I don't have time to wait for another person. I need to get to my flight before 6:30." Reader, my Aqua Master read Quarter to five! Which gives us 45 minutes of Play.

"With all due respect; I asked him. Sir, do you know what Pool is?"

"I don't give two Cents about a Pool!" He screamed. I need you to get me to my destination. Before I cancel the trip!" He added.

"Relax Jack" I spoke to myself in third person. But did this idiot just threaten to cancel the trip, reader?! He's maybe twenty minutes away from where I picked him up, and he's running late!

Like I'm going to change my route by not picking up my next customer. Especially because he decides that he wants to share a ride at a cheaper rate, well aware that he had to be at an appointment by a certain time!

Like I'm not going to keep my cash flow, flowing! Like you are placing my life in danger because you threatened to cancel the trip.

"Be my guess!" I almost thought aloud. I drove and continued to drive until I reached my next customer. And when I picked him up, I took my time dropping him off.

I hit turnpike North. Destination Newark International Airport.

After reaching the Airport the disturbed and disturbing customer climbed out of the car then slammed the door. I watched this arrogant clown walk away and I figured that was the cue for me to start making my way home. I miss home anyway.

Chapter Two

Getting nearer and nearer towards the big transition. Me and my family are putting things in order. We are doing our best to make sure that we don't underestimate anything that may require immediate attention. I didn't want to leave any rock unturned.

Being that I will be miles and miles away I want to make sure that I leave my mother in a good place. She always makes excuses about not being able to get to Church. Getting here! Getting there! So on and so forth.

"Sweetheart, I want my mom to have a car. I think I want to buy her one for her Birthday." I let my wife know. With a smile, she agreed.

"Babe just make sure that she gets something that she can afford." My wife replied. She's so straight forward. She wants things to be done in decency and in order, reader. I will have it no other way.

The only question in my head was how to explain to my mother (The Queen of the Hoagalino family) that there was a spending limit on her new car.

"The best way to explain this to her will be through the dealer." I thought.

"Bakann, you have a Birthday coming up I want to buy you a car." I told her.

"Well Praise the Lord!" She replied. But from her response, clearly, she didn't take me serious. And if she did she didn't think that she will be getting this gift soon. Little did she know her car was already worked out.

Pastor Bellamy won't be losing hair about not seeing this Queen.

I'm sitting here looking at my mother, and the joy across her face is unexplainable. I feel so good to know that as I take this journey to the height of my career she will be in a better place today than yesterday. It's even more of a blessing to know that I'm able to be a stepping stone to get her to a better place than yesterday.

Poor Boonkie (My sister) has a way of camouflaging things. Only today it creeps through her features. She's moping around probably thinking;

"Wow my brother is really leaving." But what I want her and others that may be feeling this to think about is; This move is a career move. A career jump. Yup leap of faith.

My plan reader, is to get to the "A" and let my actions speak through me.

I have a plan of helping my mother and sister get established into their own place. God Willing it's a house or something of that comfort.

I picked her up and mad my way up route 1 north. Lucky for us there was very little people in the office.

"What up Steve this here is the Queen of the family. My mother!"

"Hey mom's" He greeted Bakann.

"Steve I need you to put my mother in a nice car for less money. Maybe a $8-$10,000.00 ride." I emphasized.

Steve looked at me dumbfounded. So I continued; "I need to make sure that she's able to foot the bill when I'm gone."

After an hour or two Bakann began to release cry water. "I'm proud of the man that you have become." She whimpered. She then grabbed a hold of me and continued to whimper on my shoulder.

"I love you so much. I know that this is your destiny. And I know that Teri is the right one to travel with. Because God put y'all together."

"Just know that your mother loves you." She expressed.

"Mom, you don't have to worry about me. I'm a big boy!" I used this tactic to lighten the load.

"Boy I'm your mother. When you're 60 years old, I will worry about you. Because I will still be your mother." Bakann was holding me like her life depended on it.

Chapter Three

If you've been to this spot you're familiar with this guy. For those that are not, this guy here owns Top Golf located on Rt.1 south.

At Top Golf, y'all been on the website. They lean towards the sports and entertainment venue. Their goal is that you, your family, and friends have an unforgettable experience. Well this guy who's new in town from Iowa, Has the rights of regulation to such an establishment.

As his driver, I have the privilege to be of assistance to him and his success. After hearing my story and engaging in a little converse, let's just say he wanted in. He told me that I spoke like a guy with a wealthy Spirit. I looked at him and whispered;

"But I really am." I doubt if he understood. Only a person that serves the God that I serve, would.

Anyway, before he left my car he gave me an envelope that contained a sum of money and tickets that said WELCOME TO WEALTH as a courtesy invite to his establishment. He ended that with congratulations on your accomplishments!!!!

"Reader do I have to express how much I love tippers..."

Yes, Uber to me was a lot more rewarding of an experience than a couple of zeroes added to my account.

With Uber every day I received what I was supposed to receive from the customers. Even the ones that knew nothing about what they had for me, had to give it me. Because God said so. It can even get a little deeper than this; they just may get in the car and leave with something that I had for them. Because vice versa, as God's children He uses us the same.

Later that night during Church service. The Spirit of the Lord was having its way with the Men and Women of God. I sat back and began to praise God for the countless blessings that has been coming our way. Then it happened.

"Jack take three steps towards this altar." I got up and pardon me, excused me, my way through the aisle until I made it to the altar.

"Give me your hand." He commanded. He then grabbed hold of my hand and began to walk with me across the front of the altar;

"Jack, I know how you must feel. God has already told me. You will be a million miles away from home. You won't know anyone in Atlanta. And a bunch of other things that the devil is whispering in your ear.

But the Lord said to tell you, just as I hold your hand and walk with you down this aisle, He will be there in Atlanta to hold your hand and walk with you. He said to tell you to follow your dream, to have no fear and that He will be with you holding your hand the whole step of the way."

Reader, I snatched my hand away from the young Pastor, raised them in the air and immediately began to praise my God. Tears tailgated each other as they ran down my face.

"My God"

"Thank you Jesus!" I began to thank God for the confirmation. Not to mention the flash back of the yesterdays, Homeless, Restless, Cold nights!

Sometimes God places people in our life's, so that they can be a blessing to us. Since a boy Jessie has been praising God. He's anointed to heal and Prophesize over a person's life. This Pastor puts his hands on a person and they magically lose their legs. Some may take off running.

Today he has given me a message of confirmation that I needed to hear. So after the Prophetic word I waited until the air cleared then I walked up to him.

"Cuz, it amazes me how the Lord uses you." I whispered. His look became a stare, and he began to nod his head in agreement.

"But God!" was all he could say.

"I love you Cuz." He added. You're going to do well in Atlanta."

On the other side of the Deliverance Prayer Revival Church my sister was shouting and screaming while the Holy Ghost attached himself to her.

Jessie ran over to her and with one light tap to her abdomen he knocked her off her feet.

For the next twenty minutes, she lay dormant as if she were asleep. Talk about anointed to heal. This young man of God didn't stop there. He knocked half the Church on their behind and backs. Then began to shout himself.

I walked over to my sister helped her off the floor and whispered:

"Everything will be alright Boonk." Teri walked in back of her and grabbed her with a strong embrace. This night was an amazing anointing night. The faces seemed to be so refreshed. If no one else did, I got what I came to get. And I'm sure the others did as well.

Chapter Four

"Sweetheart for some reason this car is acting up. You know what this mean?" I questioned my wife. She got quiet. Because she already knew what that meant.

"You get a car! You get a car! You get a car!" Oprah began to cloud my thoughts.

I called my dealer and began to explain my situation. "Bob, I think I'm a need another vehicle." I chimed into the speaker of my car phone.

"Well Jack, you know who you have to speak to." My dealer responded.

After being dumbfounded for almost an hour, my wife took the wheel and decided that we will be leaving with a truck instead of the piece of cars that we've been tolerating.

Before we made it home in our new addition to the Hoagalinos, Teri made a three-picture post of how grateful we were that our God has kept His promises.

There were countless congrats. From verbal to emojis of congrats. But then it happened;

"BUY HERE PAY HERE?! LOOKS LIKE EDISON AUTO SALES TO ME!" Said an ex of mines auntie. Always remember reader, in every setting of congratulators there will always be at least one hater.

"Her AUNTIE tho!" I attempted to follow the thought of lashing out but as the CONGRATS continued to flood Teri's timeline, I saw that there was more Love than Hate. So I smiled and ignored this creep. She was who she was and my reply could never take that from her.

But my wife on the other hand, just couldn't let it sit well in her stomach. She added her name and all.

The new edition to them Hoagalinos.

"Sweetie, you couldn't begin to imagine the story behind this Glory, God is good and He is a keeper of His promises. "WHEN THE LORD JUST KEEPS ON BLESSING YOU!" She ended. LIKES began to flood that reply.

Not even an hour later the devil is still busy...

"So why didn't you tell nobody you were moving down south? And why didn't you invite anybody to your Wedding?" This was an inbox from one of my children.

"Is this your way of reaching out?" I asked her.

"I don't have your number and my phone is broken... But my questions.." She countered.

"Listen sweetie what I get from you and your siblings is nonchalant disrespect. And a cold heart of negligence. Why would I feel that either of you would care about where I am or where I am going? You are a bright girl. Be honest" I told her.

"You don't receive disrespect from me, my sisters maybe! But not me. If you feel like that's what you get, then Hey, that's how you feel.

But what makes you think that I wouldn't care that your moving down South or that you got married? That's real funny to me and last I checked you were mad because I was around my baby dad and you didn't want me over here with him because you don't like him. So you be honest" She barked.

"What y'all think, this is a game?!" I asked her.

"Here I am running for my life! You and your siblings wouldn't care if I live or died. Why act like it's such a big deal now?! You don't call me. You don't speak to me. You don't like me. I wouldn't be surprised if you didn't love me!"

"There's a Calling on my life, sweetie. And I'm heeding to that Call. I'm a dreamer that follows his dreams!"

"You and your siblings are grown now. You have no respect for life. And I'm tired of trying to prove who I am to you. I'm getting older, I can't chase you anymore. I'm sorry but I can't do it.

You kicked my back in, my wife back in. As if that person you confided in wouldn't come back to me. I mean like the list goes on.

The love that I have for you will have to be from a distance. I need people around me that knows who I am and are willing to respect me for that alone. One day you will realize who I am and what I was trying to do with you. I love you."

"How you sound? I'm not about to sit here and kiss your tail. All I asked about was your wedding and the fact that your moving. Never did I try to make it a big deal. I clearly said my phone is broken, so therefore how am I supposed to call you.

Last I checked if I didn't care I wouldn't have in-boxed you, and when did I kick Teri back in?

Teri is the only one of your little chicks that I actually liked and gave a hoot about. So get out of here. I don't know what whoever told you and I don't give a hoot! about what they told you!

You expect to get respect from someone you hardly know. How about thinking about how I feel. I gave you WAY more respect than I should have given you. You don't deserve it."

"When was the last birthday that you were there? You try to buy your kids and that stuff don't work. Money Darn sure don't make me. If you didn't notice by now I'm very independent and don't need nobody for nothing!

All you did my whole life was make false promises. Still never took us to Disney World. That's funny. What happened to me getting a car? I took a driving class for nothing. Still didn't see a car! Like F out of here. So don't ever try to say I didn't show you respect. Respect, that you didn't deserve.

"Oh yeah Love you back!" She ended. The mouth of this barely legal little girl. One would think that she's fighting someone from the streets! I apologize for her mouth reader, but this here is my baby!

"Don't ever contact me again!" I told my daughter.

This was probably one of, if not THE hardest thing for a father to say to his child. Although I may have been equipped I no longer felt that I deserved such results from trying to be a part of my children's life's. Some may beg to differ, but; THIS WAS THE HARSH TRUTH OF MY REALITY. After this crazy experience of a meeting I immediately began to pray.

"Lord there has to be something that I'm missing here. What is it that I'm doing so wrong? Please speak to me Lord!"

(REMINISCING)

{Because of you, this happened. Because of you, that happened. Because of you, I had to experience this. That!" So on and so forth!" As I read these harsh words leaving the mouth of my youngest daughter, at first I was thinking;

"Little girl you're not scared to speak to your father like that?" But I had to respect the fact that like everyone else's mind set this was her reality. Tears began to chase one another down my cheeks.}

If I would have made better decisions. Decisions like not thinking that I had to put myself on the block to make sure they ate, they were sheltered, they were clothed etc.

Just to learn that from somebody's prison I would not be able to feed them, house them, or clothe them anyway. The selfish, negligent, ignorant clown I was to waste my time and theirs, for so many years!

But unlike then today I'm here; up close and personal! Front and center.

I am bringing all of me to the table. So I will no longer fill myself up with who I should've been to them. And why? And more importantly I will no longer accept the mental abuse that follows.

(Moving along)

After learning that she was seven months pregnant and kicked in the streets once again, my wife and I decided to let her into the home that we shared with our children (Through Marriage). I had the talk with her (My Daughter). I explained to her that she was to respect me. And that she might want to listen to my suggestions.

One suggestion was; to make sure that the baby is not put in harms way. And that although the baby's father was the baby's father, this didn't negate the fact that he was not a father to his baby. So he was only allowed into my home to briefly visit.

This was until he showed me that he was ready to be a father to his child. Of course my daughter didn't understand, but my thing was that I really didn't need the spirit that followed him to follow him into my comfort zone.

Being that she lost her job, she was on her bike to get something to fill in the void. She was asked to come and work at some Ice Cream Parlor in Jackson, New Jersey. This ice cream parlor was located in a town not far from Six Flags (Great Adventure). A young lady that she apparently knew asked her to come and work there. But she had no ride, so for a couple of weeks her reliable transportation was on me. (The Dad that was never there!)

Although New Brunswick, New Jersey is about an hour away from Jackson, New Jersey (60 miles easy). And her pay wasn't enough to take care of herself. Let alone my tank and the wear and tear of my vehicle. Never once did I (the dead beat that was never there) complain about transporting her to and from work daily.

After a long night shift, she came home from work and had her first experience of a labor. Me, Teri, and my step-kids sat at St. Peter's medical hospital for hours. (Mind you reader, we all had to be at work in the morning. Some earlier than others) Just to learn that she had a false labor.

This repetitive situation became an on-going thing for the next two weeks. And each time, with no complaints we were there by her side front and center.

She was getting closer to her due date, so my wife and I decided that we would give her a surprise baby shower.

Lil Man theme is what she has been screaming. So we ran around to get the ingredients needed to bring this theme to life.

(Two weeks later, with very little money it happened.)

"Surprise!" A hand full of people showed up. Minus the two that she was the closest to and gave the most love and respect to. Not seeing these characters drew a certain look from her face, but hey life is what it is. Any way the ones that showed up made it a success.

Not long after, the baby was born. Beautiful little something too! He had more gifts than a child that has been raised by a village.

As the days passed my baby challenge everything that I was to her. Even worse everything that I was to My household, not to mention the slick talk that was getting more harsh by the day.

In return she began to rub off on the other girls in the house. because she made it look so easy, the girls thought it was okay to talk slick to the man of the house. Not long after the house was in an uproar.

So before the house became a Zoo, I spoke to a family member about the situation. And he figured that maybe we needed to have a sit down. I agreed and had a talk with daughter.

"Listen sweetie, I had this talk with you before you came here. Somewhere we went wrong, because this whole ordeal is about to go South." With a quiet tone, I addressed this to my daughter. Shockingly, she packed her things, the baby things and without notice she left.

Young adults these days are more willing to follow the trend that the streets teach them, then to follow a grounded fortress of family. But like I shared with you previously in this book, the difference between this time and the others is, I had gotten fed up with the puckering up to my children. I got fed up with proving myself to my children, and convincing them that I am more than that monster of an image that their mother painted of me.

But any way with less a week to go before I say Good bye to Jersey I receive this warranted in-box!!! Warranted because my God didn't see fit to block it!

My message to anyone that has done some things in life that had to be paid for with a prison sentence;

(Don't get stuck! People have the tendency to play on your vulnerability. Do not let people hold you hostage for the decisions you have made in your past.

The remainder of your life depends on it. Stay focused and move forward.)

And although this harsh truth is hard to bear, guess what reader, I'm Praising God anyhow! The God that I serve deserves the praise through the good, through the bad and the ugly! My God!

Chapter Five

Church flow y'all. After receiving a straight to the point Word of having order in the house of God, The Pastor began to discuss the criteria of Fasting. A Fast, called; The Daniel's Fast that had begun that morning. Forgive my ignorance to the Fast Lord, but I had been eating all day. After getting and receiving that good Word;

"Hey Teri. It's been a long time." Teri smiled and recalled where she knew the guy from. He had a direct connection to a friend of hers. Any way he shook my hand and proceeded to converse with Teri.

They were reminiscing about a hood that they both shared history in. In the back ground stood a pregnant woman who patiently waited with her head down as her baby's daddy conversed with my wife. Both she and I looked at each other. Although I thought it was a form of disrespect, I figured that I would respect the house of the Lord.

"Okay babe, you ready?" Teri finally asked me. She and her guy friend hugged each other then she and I walked away. He and his lady exchanged words. Couldn't hear everything but her facial expression wasn't too pleasant.

Reader, who has a long-detailed conversation with another woman while the mother of his child stands in the back ground. To add insult to injury the guy didn't have the decency to introduce Teri to his lady. Maybe it's me but I can clearly see why most relationships are dysfunctional and marriages end in divorce. Any way this was the harsh truth of my reality. Moving right along...

But at the end of the day it was the devil trying to block the blessings that somebody may have received from the Word.

Chapter Six

Getting closer to my dream, Yet so far away. Someone introduced me to this Live video thing on Facebook. So being that I am my own biggest supporter, I figured that I have should use every possible outlet that will aid me in getting to where I need to be. So I decided to go live with faith that I will go viral.

"INQUIRING MINDS WANNA KNOW"

"Inquiring minds want to know who this estranged guy that travels all the way to Atlanta, Georgia from New Brunswick, New Jersey to meet this Tyler Perry guy?"

"And why?"

"What is his motive?" Like every time that I post something I then sat back awaiting the response of my fans. Sometimes it amazes me how many people follow me, yet very few have a copy of my books when we meet. But then I think about the goodness of the God that I serve and the good always outweighs the bad.

90 percent of the people that I came up with, did time in prison with, or meet on the daily basis has at least one copy seated on the shelf with Jack Hoagalino written across the cover of the book.

But then the responses began to take off. One person said that they can't stop laughing. This came from a family member.

Was I surprised? Not at all. Sometimes family is the worst. My thoughts were; Is this the best you can do to show support? But I didn't take it to heart. One thing I learned is when you put yourself out there (especially as a public figure) for the world to latch on to, the critics are coming as well. From my

Big mama, I learned to make lemonade from lemons. So my reply was;

"I'm laughing with you, Cuz. All prosperity over here FAMILY!"

A close family member of mines comment seemed as if he was laughing as well. His response was;

"Boy you a fool. I wish you the best, tho. There's no fear in love. Because love is the strongest energy on this Planet. As long as you love what you do, no weapon formed against you shall prosper. Because your love for it will give you the strength to persevere through all the obstacles."

He ended with; "Love you Bro."

"Love you back." I replied. And thanks for the motivation." Some loved it, some reacted to it. Others just viewed and kept it pushing.

One thing that we can't do reader, is force ourselves on people. It's their right to accept us or reject us. If you cool, then I'm cool. In my Anthony Hamilton's voice.

Chapter Seven

It's been days since I spoke to B'more about the dog that he promised he will have for me when it was time for me to make the trip.

Being that he hasn't contacted me, I find myself reaching out to him on the daily basis. To no avail still he hasn't contacted me. I figure he's chasing the life that he leads. So I made up mind to leave him where he is. Sometimes we have to accept people's life style as their life style verses what you perceive as a life style.

I have so many things on my plate that I would be a fool to let the bs he brings to the table become my bs. So I began to make phone calls and add posts to my page that will bring attention to what I need from my Facebook family.

"Brah, I have an entire litter." Whispered an old co-worker through my inbox.

"An entire litter?!" I thought aloud. Loud enough for my wife to hear. Her reaction was what it always is. No comments reader!

Anyway, I made plans to get one, but the one for $250 and two for $450 turned into two for $650. Needless to say, that conversation ended before it took off.

Because of this I found myself reaching out to B'more again. This time I let him know that I had a few pennies for him. His response was crazy reader.

"Yo, I have a dog for you but I don't think that you're ready for this dog." This was his way of accepting the fact that I had money for him. verses him giving it to me for free. So he made plans to bring the dog to me.

While waiting for him to come through for me, I jumped into my car and turned my Uber on.

"Uber everywhere!" I began to sing as the smash hit song played on the radio.

"Good evening Sir, how are you?"

"I'm okay and yourself." The customer replied. How's your night going?"

"No complaints, God is good." I told him. I had so much on my mind that I really didn't have much to say. So I tried my best to ignore him and get him to his destination.

"So, is this a full-time job for you?" He asked. Do you do Lyft as well?" This guy wouldn't give up. So I finally gave him the conversation that he thirst for.

"I'm a writer with a dozen books that I've written and a hand full of published books. Not to mention the ones that I have in manuscript form." I told him.

I then went in with the whole showing up at Tyler Perry's studio thing.

"Wow, that's great!" He replied.

"Wouldn't advise you to show up at his studio! Well anyone's studio unannounced or uninvited." He added. You know it's interesting that you say that because I've been into the same industry for about 20 years. And it all started with being there and getting lucky. So my advice to you is that you follow your dream, and keeping your drive is important."

"Be there THE AREA he emphasized. You just may get lucky. Be there to Be Lucky!" He added.

"But as far as the relocating, Hell I relocated to Colorado just to go skiing. Yeah, I'm what you would consider a Ski Bum."

"Ski Bum?" Whatever that is reader. But okay. He likes it, guess who loves it?

It was good that I did take the time out of my busy head to give an ear to this guy. Now I have his number along with contacts for when I do touch down in Atlanta. I will be out there so just maybe I'll get lucky. I'm joking y'all I believe in God not luck. But it had a slick ring to it…

Like every time, I post something. Whether it be text, image, or video I went into my phone on my Facebook app. As I breeze through my comments, I read;

"Ha Ha, that's right Preach brother. Dream big and never stop!" This was from a close family member that most says has become estrange to the family. Rhan'heen is who he is, y'all! And can't no one take this from this brother.

But I will continue to promote this thing like I stressed in the video. With or without my audience, I will not leave a rock unturned.

My response was; "My Hitta! You know what Julie's son, you never know what part of your life will inspire another person's. Thank you!"

This brother's success has inspired me from a whole other level. If a veteran with 20 years in the Industry, 8 Albums, Hit after Hit and Multi-Platinum Artist, says it can be done then I'm listening and taking heed.

Chapter Eight

Getting closer to the day that I will say good-bye to Jersey. And the devil is so busy.

I looked into an empty cigarette pack. I moved the seal of the Newport box. To no avail there was nothing in the pack. I pulled into the parking lot of the corner store. Jumped out of the Jeep Commander and without turning the ignition off, I headed to the entrance of the store.

As I passed I said my what ups to the what ups. And kept it moving.

"Op, I need two dollars-worth of Newports."

"Where my money at?" He replied, in joke. But I knew better. He was grave serious. You see Op and I developed a relationship that involves banking.

Something like a Loan Shark. So when he asks questions like such, there's a message behind this.

"Op, I'm on my way out of the State." I informed him.

"Okay, well when you get back I will have your money!" He said that with certainty. As if I would still trust him with $5,000.

"Listen brah, I'm leaving for good." I gave him a little more emphasis. I mean he's an alright guy, and an okay friend but to give him this amount of money and travel a thousand miles away with no intention of returning. To have the expectations that he will have my money (with interest) upon return, would be so overrated on my behalf.

"Listen Op, I like you but I can't do it." I told him. And that's final. He smiled and said that he was joking.

From there, I got a click in my phone to pick this brother up in Piscataway, New Jersey. As this brother dragged his feet to the car, I can see that he was going through something that required immediate attention. The look that he wore across his face said:

Sorrow, Pain, A scream for Help! It didn't look too kosher, reader.

The way that I came up this type of look showed a sign of weakness. I am not saying that this brother was weak. But it was a look that said that he was at the edge and ready to leap. So I had no other alternative then to help this brother strengthen up.

Any way it was a look that needed some type of therapy.

"Are you okay brother?" I asked.

"Nah, I ain't alright. I think I just lost my job." He whispered. I listened as he spoke. Listening is something that I learned to hold on to, while doing time in the pen where I became The Pen.

Wow, that has a nice ring to it! This brother continued;

"I worked like a slave." He said. (After a pause) "Like a slave, I shed Blood, Sweat and Tears. Four years I slaved for this job, brah."

"FOUR YEARS!!!" He screamed. Tears were now flooding his eyes. It was normal though. If you're anything like me at a certain level of anger you may get a tear or two from me. So I understood.

I had to ask the brother; Was there anything that you could think of that could have gotten your livelihood taken from you.

"Brother I did nothing wrong." He replied. I began to smile. The brother looked at me like he was lost. So I explained to him.

"The God that I serve never takes what you need without replacing it with something better."

"Now you just told me that you did nothing to be fired. Not to mention the fact that you were an asset to the corporation. Brother listen to me when I tell you this;

"You lost nothing. You just may want to go back there and thank them personally."

Reader my God doesn't make any mistakes. I told the brother if you did everything that you were supposed to do and you were everything that you were supposed to be to that company, and they still let you go!

Brother, you have out-grown that company. Consider yourself a winner. You have just been promoted.

"If you haven't won anything this year, let me give you something a little more concrete, brother if you have no wins under your belt, you have just gotten one. Because God has a better job for you. He is preparing you for this job, brother!"

The brother who expressed to me earlier that he had no faith, was now very receptive to what I Ministered to him. Look at me calling myself a Minister! (Off the record y'all).

But yeah, I began to let him know about the upsets that I've witnessed. Whether it be from personal experiences or another person's life. The brother had tears flowing all over his jacket.

"Thank you brah!" He whispered through whimpers.

"Listen brother, I told him as I rolled the window down. You may want to go get that job. It's right at the tip of your fingertips." I ended.

Reader let's not overlook the Blessing by focusing on something we think is a setback. God only puts us through the things that He knows we will come out of. Only if we trust and have faith in Him.

So if you are faced with an unjustifiable situation, just know that God is there in the midst of that situation with you. He knows that you will come out. He has already made a way out before He put you there.

Chapter Nine

"They here y'all!" I thought aloud, as I fingered the case of the copies of my books THE SHIFT that I had shipped to me. I then created this big post as a promotion of the books I will be distributing for the next 4 days.

I then took off. Reader this is the best part of the process. I promote, they contact me, I find them, distribute and reap the benefits of my work.

"Yayyyy!" I wanted to scream. First, I made a stop at the shop of one of my biggest supporters.

"Giffy what up tho" I greeted my boy who is an entrepreneur that owns a clothing line called 99 Attributes. I apologize for interrupting your conversation. Like every time we bump heads he was having a conversation that appeared to be very intense and deep. But grounded.

"What up Sun?!" He returned the greeting. Okkkkay!" He added. His eyes were now focused on the product that I had clamped in the palm of my hand.

"Yeah man, I have 500 copies and guess how many I'm selling?"

"500" He quickly replied. That's when you know who your Day Ones are. Your Day Ones are the ones that know and respect your drive as if it were their own.

"Asap!" I countered. Like every time that I release a new book, he got his off the top. After we took a picture we made our way to the front of the store.

"Yo, I'm a reader." Whispered this brother. I don't have any money today. But I have a membership at the English Library! The French Library! The German Library!" The only Library this brother didn't name was The Corner Store Library! Lol...

Although that would have been a somewhat concrete contact network, this order wasn't about that. At least not right now. I was in the process of moving and I needed my finances to meet the requirements of the move. So every book that I ordered had a price tag on them. This order will aid me and my family in getting to the Atlanta.

"Brah, I feel you. But I need all the bread for these." I then began to shoot a live video on Face book. The video was in reference to the promotion of the release of my new project. THE SHIFT...

After the video my in-box was lit. So many people from my page began to contact me. The ones that never liked anything that I posted or released was hitting me as if they were the family that I came up with!

Yeah the books arrived just in time, y'all. After I hit the streets I got rid of maybe 10 copies, then I took it in.

Chapter Ten

As I headed back from Sayreville, I crossed the Bridge that led to Old bridge township. I view a car pull out of a driveway. It begin to creep up on me. Like most vehicles that get behind me, from my rearview mirror, sporadically I give them very little attention.

But anyway, this suburban area is where the speed limit decreases halfway through the bridge.

At a slow pace, I moved across the Bridge but noticed the closely tailing car that refused to pass on the left or the right. Then it happened;

The flashing cherries began to flash and flashed as the car sped to maybe A 15 miles per hour trail.

I quickly pulled over and patiently waited for him to get out of the car. From both sides of my car the officer approached my vehicle.

"License, Registration and Insurance." I slowly reached inside my glove compartment. I was careful not to make any sudden movements. Especially with all the wins the police has been getting lately.

People that wear my face, share the same upbringing as me, walk the same streets and survive the same poverty as me were being increased in crime, erased and never thought of again.

Anyway, from my glove compartment I revealed my documents and gave them to the barely legal Caucasian guy. I was shocked to see that he was as down to Earth and more respectful than family members I gave life.

"Sir, with all due respect were you consuming any type of substance?"

Is this guy serious? I thought. It wasn't hard for him to answer such a question. He was dead serious! and would stop at nothing to make sure that I acknowledged not only that ignorant question/accusation, but the fact that he's the boss.

What he didn't understand was; After everything that I've been through and survived, at 40 years of age, I would be a fool to entertain remotely anything that will challenge or put a strain on my career, my goals or the things that I bring to the table. Not to mention the things that I've accomplished. Besides, if I were, Why would I tell you?! I almost thought aloud.

"No officer! Not at all!" I replied. No Alcohol! No Drugs, nothing that could impair my thinking, or decision making." I assured the fresh out of the academy guy. Now I was beginning to think that this was one of those bogus Stops that happens on Tuesday or Thursday. You know that time that the city becomes thirsty for the needs to meet a certain quota before election or something that requires immediate attention.

"Okay, if I run your name will I find a clean slate?" He asked. This was usually a sign that he really didn't want to write a ticket.

"My license are clean as a whistle officer. But I am anxious to know why you pulled me over?" I asked him.

"Well, after my partner and myself observed you swerve from one side of the road to the other, my experience over the six months that I've been patrolling these streets told my partner that maybe you were under the influence. Whether it be Drinking or Drugging!"

"Not a drinker Sir! Nor am I a drugger!" I added.

As he disappeared with my documents, I began to thank God for the constant reminders of what I've been through and have come out of in one piece. And that I'm able to be a blessing to someone else's struggle with my story. How blessed we are to say that we have made it out in one piece. To God be the Glory.

After all of two minutes side bar with his partner he returned and whispered that I was clean and for me to have a good night.

"I apologize for your trouble Sir." He whispered.

"Oh and good luck with your dreams!" He added.

You know what reader, this was a reminder that no matter how big we get or feel that we have gotten, society is trained to perceive what they think we should be. And with all of their might they will hold us accountable to these images.

And of course act on it accordingly. This was another harsh truth.

Chapter Eleven

Things have been going slow in my hood. Every other trip was local. Although the trips didn't add up, I really didn't feel up to traveling through the route 1 traffic to get to Elizabeth, New Jersey. Although this is where my route usually begins, I decided to float around the hood until a trip clicked into my phone.

After hitting Wawa's I got a click. This guy who was only minutes away wanted to get to Trenton. Long trips are always good for me. The longer the trip the more money that trip costs. So of course I was game.

Twenty some odd minutes of driving, I ended the trip on North Clinton Ave. Trenton, New Jersey.

As I was coasting through New Jersey's Capitol, I decided to contact Two to let him know that I was in his hood.

When he didn't respond I pulled into Dunkin donuts to have a coffee break.

"Dunkin Donuts is lit!" I thought.

I found a parking spot and quickly made my way inside. There I ran into an older female friend well she was the older sister to a friend of mines.

"Heyyyy May" May was behind the counter working in the light of some Indian woman.

"How you doing Jack?" She nonchalantly returned the greeting. Long time! No see!" She added.

"So how you been?" I asked her. I sensed that she was a little uneasy with the unexpected meeting. But I haven't seen or heard from her in years, so I was genuinely concerned about her.

"I can't complain." She answered. I'm married, My son is doing awesome, I'm working." So on and so forth. She was excited to let me know that she was on her A GAME.

This is usually the response I get from a person that I've ran the streets with. It's called a defense mechanism. I assume that this was her way of letting me know that she's a changed person and that nothing will waver them. little did she know, I was excited for her.

Anyway after I got my coffee, it was time to hit the road again. So I asked her can I take a picture with her.

"Sure we can take a picture but you will have to take it from there." THERE, was on the other side of the counter, reader. But okay.

I got as close as I could get to the counter then I lightly touch the snap button that takes the picture.

I then reached to give her a hug. Her response was so quick with building a wall to prevent me from hugging her. That she almost made me jump.

"I don't do that." She snarled. Oh, congratulations on your marriage!" I just shook my head in agreement. And continued out the door before I experienced any more embarrassment.

To add insult to injury, as I was leaving out I can hear her whisper to her boss that I was Rhan'heen's cousin. I just smiled and kept it moving. It never amazes me at how a person will try to use a person to get the spotlight even after they direct insult.

Chapter Twelve

"Jack, I told mommy that me and Swag are going to catch a cab to the Coffee shop?"

Kay kay was on the move reader. She always had something going on. Only today she will have a culprit. These two are more like sister and brother than cousins. For years it has always been Swag and Kay kay.

"Coffee shop?" I asked. Us as parents must be careful not to just take the things that our children tell us on face value. These kids these days will tell you that they are going to Church and get caught posted up at a Strip club with the name CHURCH engraved on the sign. Yup gets that real reader.

"Yeah it's in Highland park." Coffee shop in Highland park? I thought. Well Highland park is the suburbs. And the suburbs never hurt anybody.

Teri and I got dressed. I can imagine what was going through their head now. DANG THEY TAKING US TOO!!!

"Ummm Hm!" We got dressed and headed to this coffee shop, which was located on the main strip that ran through Highland, Park. A block away there was noise smothering the streets of Highland park, New Jersey. As we pulled up to the location it was clear where the noise was coming from. We dropped them off directly in the front of the building.

"Really Jack?! Directly in front?!" Kay kay whispered.

"So this is the coffee shop they was yappin about?" Teri asked. Oh well they here now. I thought as we scanned the club like disco lights flashing and lining up with the beats.

"Call us when y'all ready." We both sang. Then kept looking back as we slowly drove away.

Later that night I was awaken by Teri. "Bae I think Swag was drinking." I listened to my wife and although this required immediate attention I had to keep calm.

Chapter Thirteen

Bright and early that next morning there was a knock at the door. A knock that beat the sunlight.

"Somebody's knocking at the door." Chimed Kay kay. We weren't used to people unexpectedly showing up at our house. May get a visitor or two once a month. Even then it's from a close family member or someone from the complex.

I slipped my pants on followed by my house slippers, I then proceeded to the kitchen to answer the front door.

"Who is it?" I asked.

"Franklin township Police" The toad voice guy answered after a brief pause. As I opened the door he began to look around me as if he was looking for someone.

"How can I help you?" I asked.

"How's it going this morning, Sir?" He greeted. But continued to eye scan pass me into the body of my house.

"No complaints here. How can I help you Officer?" I asked once again. This time I was trying to catch eye contact with the guy, who was clearly looking for someone behind me.

"My name is Officer Jason Jazz, from Franklin Township. I received a call of a missing person who is supposed to be here at this address." I looked at this weirdo and was so lost.

"A missing person? Here?!" I then saw my son Swag leaving out the back door. But I was more focused on what was in front of me.

"Yes Sir. A young lady who resides near here says that her son Swag is missing and may be kidnapped by his father." Chuckle chuckle! I almost lashed out.

"Did this mickey fickey really send the Police to my home?!" I thought. And even worse, Did this clown not understand what he just verbalized to me?

KIDNAPPED BY HIS DAD! Maybe it's me reader, but are parent's even able to kidnap their own children?

But then I began to think of how this guy had a job to do and this complaint would be part of his job description. On another note, I thought of how I would feel about me if I were her.

I mean like the audacity of you to go to prison for seven years, come home and instead of returning back to prison like the Jack Hoagalino that I know, you're on this path of prosperity and continue for the next 4 years.

Who are you to become a hood celebrity over night?! An author of not one, two but countless books that are in stores near and far, available for the world to read. Who are you to not chase me and beg me to let you back into my life?!"

At a time that most would be highly upset I began to smile. Because this was the harsh truth of my reality...

"Officer the young man that you're looking for is my son. He's right here. At times we tend to be a little selfish by overlooking the harm that such actions can play on the psych of another person's self-esteem. Sometimes the life that we lead tells us that we no longer have what it takes to continue to do what we've been perfecting for years." I whispered.

The Officer looked at me as if he were trying to look through me. My assumption is the humility I exercised to such accusations. But who knows what could be lurking in the mind of this guy whose job is to uphold the law.

"I apologize for the inconvenience, but I would have to take him back to his mother." He stressed. Reader, guess who wasn't beat?! I would never want my son to experience that ride in the back of a Police official's cruiser.

"I will take him home myself." I told him. I'm sure you'll follow me!" I added.

"Sir I'm at the end of my shift. I have one request, please don't take me on a chase." I chuckled a little. Although it sounded like the act of a sick mickey fickey it happens, so I assured him that I will not do such a thing.

My wife and family climbed into our Jeep Commander and made our way up Highway 27 South.

As we entered my son's mother's apartment complex, she comes wobbling down the stairs. Just as I thought reader, the perpetrator was drunk as a skunk. Somethings never change I told my racing thoughts.

A few words were exchanged and the Police clearly saw that she was heavily intoxicated. So I was allowed to take my son back with me.

ALLOWED TO TAKE MY SON! Wow,
The harsh truth of my reality.

Chapter Fourteen

We're on the countdown. The girls are getting all prepped for the trip. They all put their two weeks in two weeks ago, so for the past few days they've been running around to prepare for the trip.

Meanwhile I cut Uber off to meet with B'more. When he pulled up he had a chocolate dog. I summoned him into the house where I gave him a small envelope and he gave me the new edition to our family. Oh well money normally has a nice ending!

Any way She was a 13 months old Eli / Jeep Pit bull puppy that went by the name of Hershey. She was so dark chocolate, that it didn't take a rocket scientist to see where the name came from.

He took the envelope with the money. But he magically forgot the papers. Bad sign reader!

(this GIFT was a GIFT that had to be PAID for. Oh well meet B'more!) He then handed Hershey to me on a leash. She had the smell of stink steaming from her body. So me and Yolanda put her in the bath tub.

At this time we didn't have any dog shampoo, so we improvised.

"Can we use this?" Yolanda asked me. She was so excited.

"Sure we can" I told her.

"Oh myyy, I have my own doggie. I always wanted to have a dog that I can call my own." I looked at my step-daughter and was happy to see the smile across her face.

"Hold her for me so I can wash her."
She told me. The chime in her voice made
it so easy to say Yes to whatever she
requested. As an ex-head teacher at the
Goddard Children's school who would
second guess her hospitality. Even
Hershey sensed the love.

We scrubbed and scrubbed until
Hershey, (Who's name magically became
Coco) became Milk chocolate. Baby girl
was clean as a whistle. Yes reader,
Yolanda changed her name asap.

Right from home I turned Uber back
on. For those that knows Jack Hoagalino
knows that my day Literally does not
belong to me! I found myself on the road
all day. Uber was unpredictable. In order
to make money you will have to catch the
Hit (Trip request). You never knew when
your phone will hit and you will be a fool
to miss the hit.

While making my rounds with my Uber gig. "Gig" I'm cool!

But yeah, I stopped at a Dunkin Donuts located on route 1 south, the South Brunswick, New Jersey area. As soon as I entered the little convenient coffee shop, this brother graciously offered me a cup of coffee. No money y'all. If you're anything like me, you love FREE anything....

Well needless to say that I accepted that coffee; Almond milk light with Hazelnut and 3 sugars. With a smile and an extended hand he gave me the coffee. In return I gave him a copy of my most recent book called THE SHIFT. After glancing at the cover;

"Are you Christian?" He whispered.

"Yes I am!" I confirmed.

"Oh okay. And thank you. I will read." He ended. As I was leaving the store I glanced through the window and could see that his face was stuck in the body of my book. Reader, every Author's dream is to witness a person reading their book. Today I witnessed that.

I began to smile and thank God for having mercy on this brother, because I know that there was something in this book that may be a blessing to his life his family's life. Or someone that he's connected to some way or another.

If nothing else, to add another level to his faith. Something that most of us as people tend to lack in the process of our growth.

Chapter Fifteen

So today is my big day. Finally taking my CDL test again. I began to think about my loved ones.

The closer I come to my success, the more I see the effect my transition is having on the ones that are closest to me. It's like they are beginning to stray away.

Little advice; Don't let my success make you feel less than. My intentions are to give you the visual that the things that you see as being far away are actually closer than they appear.

I say this because when certain people see certain things happen in certain parts of their life's or of that person they came up with! Ran with! Did time with! So on and so forth, they tend to see the growth and feel like you've outgrown them and they no longer have a place in your life. And this is usually true IF you stagnate your own growth and development! HINT! Get the message.... LET MY SUCCESS IMPOWER YOU! NOT DEVOUR YOU!

Whenever you are ready just say yes and know that the God that I serve accepts those Foxhole Prayers too. (Those little in the closet, the bedroom, even at the prison you're temporarily housed at.)

I remember those tough days in the penitentiary. (on the tier, in the yard, mess hall etc) But when my Bunkie left the room to go to yard. And it was me all alone with my true self! The gangster in me went out the window. This is the time that I used to cry out to my God. The time that I used to beg to be home with my family. To beg for my visits. To beg to see another day! Although we wear them faces that looks good when we are around certain people but I had to realize that my God was bigger than those people! He knew me better than those people! I have my trust in Him not those people! And eventually He will create a scenery that will have those people Praising Him while they entertain the ones that they praise. Especially those people! This thing is real y'all!

As I make my way up Interstate Highway 95 North I began to think about the goodness of the God that I serve.

I get to DMV in Lodi, New Jersey and confidence would be an understatement to describe the way that I was feeling.

After three hours of waiting to perform my pre-trip inspection I finally get to the truck, just to learn that I have no license on my person.

"Darn! Darn! Darnnnn!" With only hours left before we say good bye to Jersey, so many things began to confront me one at a time.

Not only did I not have license to take my test. But having no license to drive back down this Highway maybe 100 miles, 15-20 towns, State Police barracks, so on and so forth, I'm screaming NOOO!!!

But yeah, I haven't done this type of nonsense since I played in the streets. All I could think of was how my God promises to have my back! And I began to praise Him!

"Lord I ask that you shield me. Block any obstacles, Lord, that may be in my path as I travel down this highway. So that I can make it to the closest DMV." I left that alone and start thinking about other things that has been taking place in my life. Like moving out on faith alone. Like making plans to show up at Tyler

Perry's fortress. Like having no one to turn to when/if things get rough. The list goes on.

I began to praise Him more. This time I was more direct.

"Lord I'm playing my part. I'm a husband to my wife. A father to my girls. A provider to my family. Consistent writer to my fans. So on and so forth. I'm at the height of my dream Father. I'm at the mercy of You today, Father. I'm begging for You to make THIS one a little easy for me and my family." Suddenly this day began to take a turn.

"What up Leon?" I spoke into the receiver of my car phone.

"What up Neph? What you doing?" He chimed.

"Praising God like never before!" I told him.

"Good" He immediately replied. Because God just set you straight. I was lost reader. But he continued.

"Did you know that we had family in Atlanta?" He asked. I mean FAMILY family!" He added.

"Nah I didn't know that." I told him.

"Well I was speaking to one of our family members that lives in Atlanta. And after I let her know that you were on your way and that you will be staying in the hotel until you find jobs and a place to relocate." Reader as he was speaking, once again tears began to water up in my eyes. One may say this guy is always crying. But for me, it's more like I CAN FEEL today...

Most wouldn't understand what it means to actually be able to Feel. After being Heartless! Ruthless! Thoughtless for years and years, to finally be able to feel is a beautiful thing.

"Family member?! Atlanta?! Wow my God!" Is all I could mustard up.

"But yeah, she says call her and she will let you and the family have the whole half of the house. Free of rent, Jack!" Tears began to flow and flow and I continued to Praise God.

My God makes promises to his humble faithful servants. A little faith reader, will take you a lot further than you could have taken yourself a whole lifetime.

Chapter Sixteen

Happy birthday to Yolanda!!! Like most times, I wait til the last minute to do things. So if you're anything like me you will know that I didn't do the shopping for gifts thing. But my family is a little different. We create fun time! Family time! We bring things like Birthdays to life. So they made plans to go out to eat.

In my head, I was screaming "Yayyy!" We ended the night at a Mexican restaurant called "On the Border." Needless to say, that On the Border was located on the border of Highway 1 South, and Highway 18.

Even with very little money to play with everyone was so excited as if we just hit the lottery. We laughed. We joked. We celebrated like family. And the hosts were so hospitable.

While there we got a call from that family member that Leon was talking about. That cousin that I never knew existed. At the half a century mark, she appeared to be down to Earth. So happy she was to be a Hoagalino! We talked as much as our ears could stand until I then decided to respectfully end the call.

My phone was already at 1%, so I let her talk until the phone died.

"Babe did you just hang up on her?" Of course not reader. I just let the phone die.

"The phone died babe." I told the truth.

"Whatever. You play too much!" She chimed.

"We'll call her back." I informed my wife.

From there we made our way back to the house just to learn that Coco threw up all over the couch and rug.

"Ughhh!"

"Ahhh!" the girls screamed. But how could you get upset with someone or thing that knows not what they have done. Or is doing. I found a bucket, I added hot water, with disinfectant and bleach I went in just like Bakann taught me. That night ended with a prayer.

Chapter Seventeen

LAST DAYS IN JERSEY! Me and my wife are running around like chickens with our heads cut off. We're trying our best to please everybody. Being that this was a move of faith that God Himself ordered, authored, approved, we figure that we will leave everything materialistic that we owned in New Jersey for whoever it is that needed it.

"Boonk, Mom, I have a bunch of things here at this house that I'm not taking." My mother and sister wasn't too concerned about the things that we were leaving. I later learned that they were more concerned about her brother leaving. Her son leaving. But they still agreed to take the things.

Now I'm like; How will I get these things to my mother and sister. Mom is a lot older and sick at times. She can't carry much. And my sister, who has a handful to tend to. Couldn't sit down long enough to count money. (Lol) Together they couldn't do too much. So this meant that I will have to get these things to them.

"Okay I need y'all to be at my house Thursday at 3 o'clock in the afternoon. I want y'all to get first dibbs on everything that y'all feel that you may need." (days notice reader.)

Meanwhile I began to make calls to other family members to see if anyone else could use a table, a dresser, a bed, a wall unit. So on and so forth. Teri and the girls moved things, disposed of things, cleaned things and thangz!

If your family is anything like mines, they are never on time. But anyway 3 o'clock Thursday turned into that morning that we were leaving. I decided to send a warning text.

"Make sure that you're home in a couple hours Boonk." Was the text that I sent. Being that my mother was routed in the opposite direction I gave her a little more time to prepare for my arrival.

"I'm sorry brother. But I had a lot of running around to do with your mother." Boonk told me. She then walked through the door and started to inventory everything in sight.

When Boonk finally left Leon came through with his wife (Reese). After us not speaking for months I decided that to let things nonsense continue I will only be blocking my blessings. Because to hold a grudge with someone, especially over something that holds very little merit in that person's life or family's life (for that matter) will only put a strain on a person's mental, emotional, and spiritual growth.

"Hey Reese, give me a hug." I whispered. She climbed out of the car and with tears in her eyes, she embraced me as we whispered to each other that we will miss the other and we expressed physical and verbal apologetic energy.

Leon who was in the background began to release cry water as well. Leaving always brought out the true feelings of a loved one. But it didn't matter, for me it was more like getting to the point of closure. So closure is what I got. Anything that takes place after this to God be the Glory!

After I gave them what they came to get, me and my team closed the door to our old apartment, we made a circle, grab hands, and began to send them prayers up for safe travels. My wife took off in prayer, I added a few things. But Yolanda took us home and closed us out.

As we made our way out the door and to the doors of each vehicle, I grabbed Coco and headed to the back where the cage was, but because we were in for a long ride, I decided to let her keep me company...

Before we hit the highway, I decided to stop by to see Bakann. As normal she was down and out. But what really caught my attention, was the face that the baby (My Niece) wore. She wore a face that said that she lost her best friend.

"What's wrong baby?" I asked. While I awaited her response;

"Ma, Uncle Jack is leaving. Ma he leaving for good." Bakann added. My niece just sat quietly observing what she found hard to digest.

Teri is the best. She leaned over to my niece and along with a hug she planted kisses on her little red cheeks.

I walked to my mother and as we embraced she found it hard to let go. It was a clear indication that she didn't want her only son to leave. But God ordered this move so I had to follow through with this one.

Once again, my wife is the greatest. She inched over to me and mom and closed her embraced around the both of us.

"Okay bae, it's time to hit the road." I chimed into the ears of my wife.

"Get over here Kay Kay. Yolanda, you too Isha!" Bakann chimed. Each one made their way back and after hugs and kisses we hit the road. Destination; Tyler's town. Black Hollywood.

Chapter Eighteen

"G'ma!" I almost screamed aloud. How could I forget to stop by my G'ma's house before leaving?

"I have to run to my grandma's bae." I quickly made a right from Highway 27 on to Franklin Boulevard into Franklin township. I headed towards a little projects called the Grove.

I pulled in through the back of my grandma's complex. I climbed out of the truck and grab Teri by the hand as we made our way through the drizzle of rain that was coming down.

(KNOCK! NA-NA KNOCK! KNOCK! KNOCK! KNOCK!)

"Baaaaby?" She squeezed through her beautiful voice. It always amazes me how everybody who's house that I visit knows my knock by the knock.

"Yes Mama, it's me." I answered. Like every time she opens the door she was all smiles.

"Hey Mama." Me and my wife chimed in chorus. I didn't just want to drop the load on her. So I created a level of comfort before I informed her that I was on my way to Atlanta.

"Baby are you hungry?" She asked. I smiled.

"No Mama, I'm not hungry." G'ma thinks that everybody that steps into her home has a hunger spell!" Lol. Hunger spell Jack??!!!

But this was not the case reader. "So how are you feeling?" I asked her.

"I'm okay baby. The question is how are you feeling?" She countered.

As much as we try to hide what's going on with us. Whether it's how we are feeling or what we are thinking, the one's that raised us or helped raised us in this matter, knows exactly who we are and most of the time what's going on with us.

9 times out of 10 it's written all over our faces. But yes, she knew that something was up. So I just came out and told her.

Telling her was a very emotional setting. We embraced and held onto each other for the next 10 minutes as we shed cry water on each other's shoulder.

"Mama, no matter how far away that I am, I will never forget who you have been to me and more importantly who you are to me. You have done things for this man that stands before you that no one else has ever done.

With a smile, I remember the first bike that I ever climbed on to was a gift from you. I remember the Walkman that you gave me with it. And the words;

"Jack Jr. promise Grand mama you won't have these headphones playing while you ride this here bike?" We both laughed at this.

We reminisced about other things like how I sang in the choir. And the most hilarious moments like the time that I baptized myself. To God be the Glory...

(REMINISCING)

During church service, at the tender age of 4, a child never really pays attention to caution signs for open waters.

So while at Church in Neptune, New Jersey little Jack Hoagalino made his way through the pulpit to the drummer set which was located by the pool.

Jack just continued to make a way to the drummer set. While making his way he can hear commotion.

As the commotion came closer Jack felt cool water over his young body and the taste of salty water in his mouth. Not to mention the burning sensation in his nostrils.

Jack was grabbed by the back of his suit jacket and yanked out of the water.

As Jack got the focus back in his ears and eyes he could hear the noise of clap and as he turned around he saw that everybody was doing what he now knows as praising God for the baptism of himself.

But anyway, back up to date, G'ma played a big part of who I am today, reader.

"I love you Mama and I'm going to miss you." I whispered.

"Here too baby!" If you knew my G'ma you know that her response to I love you is HERE TOO or THE SAME HERE BABY!

Anyway me and the wife made our way back to the truck where the rest of our little team seated in their vehicles.

Chapter Nineteen

Hours into the trip, while traveling down the New Jersey Turnpike Highway 95 South, once again Coco regurgitated everything inside out and into the cup holder of the console of the car.

I was upset. More for how my wife would react to this happening in her car, than the fact that this took place in my presence. I pulled to the side of the interstate and stood speechless as I figured out a way to fix this grave issue before explaining this to my wife.

I don't know if you reader, have ever been in this situation but picture a mouth feces filling up the cup holder that will be used to hold your coffee, your tea, your juices, or what have you. Then it happened.

"Babe, what's wrong?" She chimed as she drove pass with her eyes zeroed in on the situation. The crazy thing was with her driving my truck she was towering down over us, so it was easy for her to look into the car. Instead of trying to hide;

"Sweetheart Coco threw up on everything." I told her. She began to shake her head.

Being that I'm pulled to the side of the highway I decided to let her out to use the bathroom. Just like a dog, she jumped out and stood in one spot with her beautiful eyes locked on mines.

"Really?! Really?!" I thought aloud. I then proceeded to clean up the slop.

"Help me Lord!!!" I whispered.

After spraying, wiping, rearranging things I figured that this was not going to be good enough. So I told my wife that we needed to find the closest rest stop.

A mile down the road, we pull into a rest stop. While vacuuming the cup holder, I ran across my first sale out of State. We were now in Richmond, Virginia. This brother and his family asked my step-daughter to take a picture of him and his family. That was my cue to promote THE SHIFT.

"Here brother add this to that picture." I screamed. The brother smiled and took my book. After Yolanda took his pictures I went in with how we're in the process of a move of faith and how he will be a part of this move. five minutes or less he was leaving with THE SHIFT.

"I'm trying to be a part of The Shift too." Chimed one of his family members.

"Thank you" I said to the family member, Enjoy the read." I ended gracefully.

(Back on the road)

We were in route to having good timing, but then the rain began to cover the windshield. I watched the rain come down and began to speak things into existence.

"Lord I ask that you cover all three vehicles as we fight our way South of the border." The Lord answered my prayer, but twenty minutes later it began to pour down again. I just continued to make my way to Tyler Perry. Besides, my family was determined to get to their family.

It was time to gas up again. By this time we were less than an hour away. After getting gas we stopped at a Walmart in South Carolina.

"If you don't mind can I bother you for a minute?" I asked this young lady. After being familiar with her not wanting to be bothered attitude I redirected her to the wife. Over the years I learned the women can relate to women better than men.

"Bae, you get the honors of introducing this young lady to THE SHIFT!" Amazingly with no hesitation, my wife introduced me as if she was me. She promoted my book so well, that she could've fooled someone that didn't know any better to believe that she was the writer of such a gift to mankind.

"Maam, my husband has written this book with his heart and soul. He authors a dozen already. And has plenty more to come."

"You just may want to be a part of this journey!" It didn't take much more than this reader. After the spill Teri gave the young lady, her short arms dug deep into her pockets. Lol.

"Thank you sweetie, But I have one more request; I need you to help me promote this thing by taking a picture with the book that you just purchased so that I can let my Facebook family know who's supporting me here in the South." She had no problem getting in front of the camera. In fact she struck a pose like she was getting paid to.

After Teri and I thanked her we were on to the next.

"Hello young lady, have you ever heard of THE SHIFT?" I asked the elder lady that was maybe 20 years younger in features.

"Can you tell me about the shift?" She questioned. With an unreadable smile, she then patiently awaited my response.

"I can explain the shift to her bae." Once again Teri came to my aid. After she informed the lady about my book the lady was digging into her purse!

"Wait brother, I see a series of 2 books. No 3-4!" She began to prophesize.

"You dear, You are his editor." She commanded my wife. And that meeting that you look for, look forward to it. But on God's divine timing this meeting will take place!"

"No sweetie, I can't let you pay for this book." I insisted that she have a copy, free of charge. You are a blessing in disguise." I whispered.

I would usually say that she knew nothing about the blessing she was to me and mines. But she was definitely a Godfearing woman that didn't mind living and dying for God. So I know that it was God and only God that showed up and made this meeting possible.

Sometimes we need to hear things like keep pushing. You're going to make it. Don't stop chasing your dreams. So on and so forth. So I thank God for the people that he direct towards my life that can be or become a blessing. Thank you Jesus.

Chapter Twenty

Finally we are here. Here in the land most known for opportunity. Some call it Black Hollywood.

"We here y'all!" We chimed. We decided to get the ball rolling asap. Being that we were out of our element, we contacted someone that was more knowledgeable.

"Hey mom, we herrr-ee." Teri chimed to my mother-in-law, who was already a resident of the A. She said that she will be there in 10. Just like she said she was there in 10 minute. On sight she and Teri embraced. And the tears began to fall from the eye lids of Teri.

Mom was more cordial than Teri. Never seen my wife so emotional! Today was different. But being familiar with what they didn't share it was amazing to see the embrace that they shared. It didn't stop there reader. The nieces, the aunties, the cousins all ran to each other like runaways being reunited.

"Thank you Uncle Jack." Ciara screamed.

"Thank you?!" I questioned.

"Thank you for bringing my auntie to me." She continued.

"Yeah cause, she wasn't coming on her own!" Salina added. Salina is Salina y'all. Out spoken, just like Kay kay. Even if it gets her jumped on.

We began to run around with intents of getting the needed credentials, so we can move into the house that my God promised us. And get situated with everything that follows. License, Post office box, Bank info. Due to lack of employment we still haven't gotten pay stubs. When we were turned around at Motor vehicles, things began to get a little overwhelming. But we managed to get what we needed. Finally we were ready to look at the house.

I put the address into the navigation. After an half hour drive the navigation lead us to a town called Decatur in Georgia. We get to the house that we've been kicking and screaming about getting the credentials to move in, and the house which appears to be a nice fit on Zillow, magically shrunk a couple sizes, and once inside, This beautiful Zillow advertisement transformed into the haunted house itself.

My thoughts were; "ZILLOW Y'ALL PLAY TOO MUCH!"

I thought about the family member that reached out through text to help me and my family get stable. And decided that now was the time to call her.

"Oh hey cousin, you down here already?" She spoke into the phone. (Bad sign reader). But to God be the Glory. So I told her yes my family and I are here.

"Well, I have to get this place straightened up. I don't want to have y'all here with no beds and food and stuff. Shoot y'all will never be talking about this Hoagalino on Facebook!" She added. Her mouth is what needed some organizing, redirection, cleaning and thangz. It wasn't the living conditions that she was trying to hide, reader!

"But any way make sure y'all contact me tomorrow, because I have a lot of running around to do. Shoot I'm a Hoagalino too! You know how we do Jack!" I just chuckled.

We decided that we would get a room until tomorrow and hit her in the morning like she said.

The next day she's in Alabama. Later that day we get a text that she's still at work. Then she's tired. So on and so forth.

NOTE: Watch the people that bite off more than they can chew, Reader. I call this talking because you have lips.

This was a bad start and I didn't want my family to be inconvenienced nor did I want them to be of any inconvenience to someone else! How does it look for a man to travel miles away with his family tagging along with thoughts that that everyone will be safe and secure when we get to our destination reader, only to find out that we're in a worse place than we were! Bad look reader! But this was my Harsh Truth...

Moving forward, the wife and I began to find the smallest things to argue about. The girls had attitudes because of the condition of being cramped up in the little 10x12 Motel room.

Although Teri was prayed up, sanctified and filled up, I sense that she had a little "I had enough!" going on herself.

Chapter Twenty-One

The next morning, we left the Motel 6 and spent a day at Tammie's (Sister-in-law) house.

"Who want some Pork chops!" One of the girls asked.

"Who want Pork chops?!" I almost thought aloud. You know your boy ain't turning nothing down but his collar.

Salina cooked and Isha brought it to me. With Isha the hospitality has TURNT up (Yup I'm hip!) since we got to the A. It was her hospitality that would get her pockets filled with a few pennies or something.

"Thanks Esh! Esh! Esssh" I showed my appreciation to my step-daughter Isha. As I was feeding my face this tasty pork chop, I began to think about where we will be lying our heads in the next few hours.

"Bae, let's just stick to the script. God got us." Teri said with a stern eye. As I turned to catch eye contact with my wife I saw that mom was seated in her most comfortable posture with none other than THE SHIFT wrapped around her full face. I just sat back in awe, as I watched the magnetic attraction that my book muscled out of my mother-in-law's interest. Teri and I caught eye contact and shared a discreet smile.

Got the license switched, tags switched. We ready. That night we ended up getting a room for the week.

"Gotta get this Uber thing off the ground, bae. I heard that Uber is 10 times the profit in Atlanta, verses New Jersey, so I'm excited to get settled." I told my wife.

"Not to mention the network of people that you will come across and be able to use as contacts. Contacts that may get you to Tyler Perry's studio." My wife added. She always had a mission to match mines. She's the best.

Chapter Twenty-Two

I'm in WOW mode right now reader. The premiere for the New Edition story is taking off tonight.

Not only did I not see this coming, the killer is that one of my little cousins is starring as Michael Bivins. My ancestors have a serious line of talents. The Hoagalinos are to the roof in this industry.

Me and the wife sat in our Motel 6 place of residence (ATL bound) we glued ourselves to the TV from start to finish. An amazing actor this guy is. My wife who wasn't too familiar with this side of the family, like myself was excited to see another Hoagalino that has made it. And not just make it. He made it big!

This was a sense of motivation for us all over again.

It was then that I got that call from Kenny (Dad to the Hoagalino movie star) "Cuz you tuned in?" He chimed with excitement.

"You know I am." I replied. Everybody from the East coast to West is tuned in! They better be. Because the wife and I are feet up loving this episode." I told him.

"Hey cuz." He screamed to Teri. With a smile, she returned the greeting.

"Cuz, I've been following your story on THE BOOK. Keep pushing, Tyler just may find you before you find him." He said this with sincerity.

This side of them Hoagalinos has always been the stay employed. Never without a job, type. And hands down God fearing family members since the craddle.

But music was his thing, His father's thing! So this is a drive he had coming up that rubbed off on his children. Now the son is on the big screen. It was clear that his drive is a drive that took off years before his time. Let the legacy continue.

There's nothing like family that grows together. I tell my children all the time. It's better to be with me, then to be without me. They don't hear me tho. "Daddy gone wild" By Zachery A. Hoagland tells that story.

But as I watch the ending of this amazing New Edition story I begin to envision my own stories taking off in front of the camera, one by one.

1. Jack Hoagalino. (Who was a low budget street hustler, chasing the life of the heart of a female that didn't know what to do with his breed of person. Trying to keep up with this female sent him back to prison)

2. Unleashed (Is when Jack Hoagalino was released and ready for change)

3. Hoagalino The Pen

4. Pay Attention

5. My Porsche

6. Fruit and Labor of Bakann

7. The Shift (The awaken! The Movement towards success)

I apologize reader, sometimes I drift off when I think about the work that I put in with the pen.

Chapter Twenty-Three

Today I'm shopping around at different Colleges with intentions of getting approved for a speaking engagement. Or possible Meet and greet Book signing.

A Historical place called Morehouse (All Male College). In the same radius set another very prestigious African American College called Spellman (All Female College).

These HBCUs are institutions of higher education in the United States that were established before 1964 with the intention of primarily serving the African American community. But have always allowed admissions to students of all races.

I walked into the Morehouse University to see a very impressive picture of our very own 44th President Obama himself. He was conducting a speech to the graduates about not having time for excuses. Although he was a graduate of Columbia University and Harvard Law, it's clear that he stays active in Colleges like Morehouse and Spellman.

But on another note; Besides the inspirational picture of OB, there was an environment of I CAN flooding the campus, and the surrounded area. The faces on the instructors said; I have a PhD in ____, which takes care of my day job. I'm going to night school for my Masters in____!

"Hey what's going on money. I'm looking for the student center." I asked this young African American kid with chinky eyes and a pair of prescription glasses. It didn't take a rocket scientist to know that mom lived on the edge. Lol, but I'm serious!

Anyway, I figured that he would be aware of what is where and who can be contacted to aid me and direct me in the direction that I need to be in.

"What's good, OG?!" He replied. That funny looking building over there, walk through the doors and ask to speak to Coretta. She should be able to help you." He ended.

My boy had more swag than them Jersey hittas I came up under. But any way, like he said I walked through the doors of the funny looking building. Inside there was more than enough help.

Instead of getting the table for the book signing, I was introduced and invited to an event called the CIAA. From the information I received this event takes place once a year. The young lady said that celebrities of all genres, will be floating around.

"Make sure you bring as many books as you can." Was the last words that left the young lady's mouth.

Chapter Twenty-Four

Me and my family have been here in the A two weeks now. And still haven't found a Church home. I sat on the edge of the bed and the card that the woman of God gave me and my wife just stood out like a red thumb.

"Bae, what do you think about visiting the Church on the flier that the Prophet gave us while in South Carolina. My wife grabbed the card and read the location.

"Babe I think this is the Church that Savannah is speaking at this afternoon."

Come to find out this was the same Church that Savannah and Jerome was supposed to be visiting.

I climbed out of my Queen size bed and quickly slipped my Shell toe (ADIDAS) sneakers on my feet. I then grab Coco's leash and we headed to the door to get our daily walk. Like every time she gets out of the cage she was so excited.

"Ay girl! C'merrreee!" I greeted my happy go lucky Eli Pit bull. She ran to me jumped into my chest, she then ran to the door which was cracked open. When she had enough room to get out, she dashed down the hall for about twenty rooms. It was irritating and funny the same. Instead of getting upset I found humor in that and chuckled for the next 10 minute.

Finally, I got her through the hallways and out of the front door. There she found her own lane. Two steps before the exit she squatted down and used the bathroom all over the floor. I was furious. But when she gave me that puppy look I was done. I just called her name and directed her to the field. She had a defecation situation then we were back to the room.

I get back in the room Teri and the girls were all prepped and ready for the Word.

We all left as a family, stopped at Tammie's house and in two cars we made it to a church that I later learned was on the Gospel radio station.

The first five minutes tears began to flood my eyes and squeeze out cry water.

"Lord this is exactly where I need to be." I shouted. The young pastor was speaking about what his God meant to him. The goodness of the God that he served. And how this was the season for the shift. The season for things that normally take place to make a shift.

After he let his heart lead him to a song that everyone at the church knew by words.

Then there was this brother that came to the stage wearing the same T-Shirts that the entire Church wore. This shirt read: I LOVE MY CHURCH It didn't take a rocket scientist to figure out why.

I don't know if you're familiar with Bishop W. Murphy! Well he's the pastor that sings "Praise is what I do" "It is working" and "You are my strength." Just to name a few. Well he was the Pastor of this enormous church.

After singing one of his most talked about songs, IT'S WORKING he went into his sermon. "I'm talking to someone that is seated right next to you, Sister! Brother!" He began.

"Yes, this person will be the voice of the people. This person will be able to make decisions in legislation."

"Do you hear me, LEGISLATION decisions family. This person will change the poverty of the world."

"This person wherever you are, come to the altar." As this man of God spoke these things into existence I threw my hands in the air and claimed the Prophesy over my life.

"This person needs a church home." Before he even got the words out of his mouth, I jumped up and made my way to the front of the altar. While standing there listening to his fluent prophesy, he whispered;

"Brother you didn't come alone. You brought a family with you. Brother go get your family." He whispered.

I made my way back to the aisle where my family was and walked them up to the altar.

"Okay ladies, this is the Church God has set aside for us. This is where we will be praising the Lord." Every one of my ladies made their way to the altar and was ready to send those praises up.

"Praise the lord brother, sister. Sisters!!!" Greeted the well-dressed guy at the altar.

"God bless you Sir!" Chimed my wife. The girls all smiled.

"Such a lovely family you have brother!" Whispered another.

"Thank you brother. Thank you!" I countered. Such a lovely team I do have if I do say so myself, Reader. I admire my wife and my ladies.

The entire experience I had a feeling that came over my body. This feeling was stuck on me. I call this feeling the Holy Spirit.

There we were embraced and instructed to the back where we began registration for our new home.

I couldn't thank God enough, reader. Even with the devil at work only minutes later he couldn't stop these blessings.

"Baby cakes, I would live in the house of God if I could." She meant that reader. Wherever the spirit of the Lord is, is where you will find my wife.

The Last Chapter

"To the right. To the right Jack." Kay kay almost screamed. As I looked in the direction that her eyes directed us to, who was there seated, clean as a whistle with a bright Kool-aid smile across his face?!

I got out of my seat. "No babe, Divine timing!" My wife interceded. Besides, you can't just get up and move around while the Pastor is speaking." She whispered, while grabbing a hold of my arm. But I was determined to get to this guy.

He was definitely in his comfort zone. The handful of body guards wouldn't have it no other way. The smallest one caught eye contact with me. It was clear that he caught the commotion. But he remained seated.

Before service ended he was in route with his entourage. So the movement screamed that it was time for me to move. Needless to say, I began to move and my family was on my heels.

"Mr. Perry Mr. Perry!" I screamed through the fenced in by three bodyguards, Tyler.

"How you doing brother?" He greeted with an extended hand.

"Mr. Perry, I traveled from New Brunswick, New Jersey specifically to meet you." As I was speaking;

"Dream do come to life brother follow your dream!" He then disappeared into his army of bodyguards.

Now panting out of my sleep, from yet another nightmare that seemed so real!!!!

All I could think was; Jack we need that, Sit down. But to think that this is almost impossible to be able to create this atmosphere is the harsh truth of my reality

Greetings my family, I hope you enjoyed the read. Coming soon....

"WELCOME TO WEALTH"

Foreword

"Good evening Ladies and Gents. Today I have a special guest with me. This guy here goes by the name of The Pen."

"Jack The Pen Hoagalino who is an author of not one, not two but numerous books. This amazing guy courageously picked his family up and traveled from New Brunswick, New Jersey. Miles and miles away to Georgia to meet Tyler Perry, right at his Estate. Literally, he went to the doorstep of Tyler's studio."

"Ladies and Gentlemen meet The Pennnnn!" She screamed. As I made my way to her stage tears began to leak from my eyelids. After embracing Oprah like she was one that raised me;

"Mr. Hoagalino, So you travels all the way to Atlanta, Georgia from New Brunswick, New Jersey. My audience would like to know why? Tell me all about this move Sir!" She then sat quietly and patiently awaited my response.

"Well Ms. Winfrey, First and foremost it's an honor and a Privilege to finally be able to have a seat on your couch. To be seated in front of such an audience."

"Thank you Thank you!" She quickly replied. Tell me more…."

ACKNOWLEDGEMENTS

First I would like to thank my Lord and savior. Jesus Christ! My amazing wife who is motivation. And my loving family.

Special shout out to my Daughter Kay kay. Who's always there front and center!!! Thank you for your expertise... Last but not least Mr. Tyler Perry himself for acknowledging such a guy!

Sincerely

"The Pen"

Contact Info:

WEBSITE: Jackhoagalino.com

 # (732) 309-0208

Made in the USA
San Bernardino, CA
10 June 2017